SAKE

S A K E

A MODERN GUIDE

by Beau Timken and Sara Deseran
Photographs by Scott Peterson

CHRONICLE BOOKS
SAN FRANCISCO

Library of Congress Cataloging-in-Publication
Data available.
ISBN: 0-8118-4960-0

Manufactured in China
Book design: STRIPE [Jon Sueda, Gail Swanlund,
    Jeremy Landman & Katie Hanburger]
Prop stylist: Emma Star Jensen
Food stylist: Kevin Crafts
Special thanks to Jackson at Tampopo/Dandelion
    for providing us with beautiful props for
    photography
    Tampopo/Dandelion, San Francisco.

Distributed in Canada by Raincoast Books
9050 Shaughnessy Street
Vancouver, British Columbia V6P 6E5

10 9 8 7 6 5 4 3 2 1

Chronicle Books LLC
85 Second Street
San Francisco, California 94105
www.chroniclebooks.com

To all of my girls.

—BT

TABLE OF CONTENTS

9   INTRODUCTION

13   Chapter 1: THE HISTORY OF SAKE IN JAPAN

19   Chapter 2: SAKE GOES GLOBAL

23   Chapter 3: SAKE RITUALS

27   Chapter 4: HOW RICE AND WATER MAKE SAKE

37   Chapter 5: TASTING, SELECTING, AND SERVING SAKE

47   Chapter 6: SAKE VESSELS: WHAT TO DRINK OUT OF

51   Chapter 7: FIFTY SAKES TO TRY

73   Chapter 8: FOOD, MEET SAKE. SAKE, MEET FOOD.

75   Lotus Root Chips
76   Cashews with Curry Salt
77   Sweet Potato Fries with Soy-Sugar Glaze
78   Lemongrass and Sake-Cured Gravlax
79   Miso-Marinated Black Cod in Lettuce Cups
81   Ahi-Mango Poke with Wonton Chips
82   Roasted Chicken Wings with Garlic and Ginger
83   Crab and Grapefruit Salad with Fried Shallots
85   Grilled Beef Kebabs with Cucumber-Carrot Slaw
86   Sake-Steamed Clams with Ginger
88   Edamame Salad with Shiso and Meyer Lemon Vinaigrette
89   Fettuccine with Shiitake Mushrooms and Pancetta
90   Serve-Yourself Sushi Tacos
93   Roasted Pork Loin with Cranberry-Ginger Chutney
94   Risotto with Sake, Hazelnuts, and Lemon

R
E
C
I
P
E
S

97   Chapter 9: SAKE COCKTAILS

R
E
C
I
P
E
S

98   Pineapple- and Ginger-Infused Sake
         Chili-Infused Sake
99   Melon- and Mint-Infused Sake
         Kaffir Lime–Infused Sake
100 Summer of Love
         Persimmon Passion
         Orange Blossom
103 Sweet Nothing
         Tamarindo
         Tropical Cloud
104 Cranberry Float
         Citrus Mistress
107 Hot Sake Toddy
         Cucumber Zinger
         Paradise Island

108 Pom-pom
         Sake Sangria
110 Tamari Mary
         Geisha's Delight
111 Fruit Cocktail
         Plum Good
         Ginger Snap
113 Lemon Sparkler
         Sake-rita
         Sake Julius
114 Tokyo Elevator
         Sake-jito
         Pear Flair
116 Dew Drop
         Tango Twist

117 ACKNOWLEDGMENTS
118 INDEX
120 TABLE OF EQUIVALENTS

INTRODUCTION

SAKE CALLED TO ME in the strangest of places—in the early 1990s in a small, dark sushi bar in Cape Town, South Africa, where I was well lubricated on what I thought was proper sake. My experience to date with "rice wine" had consisted of superheated sake served from small jugs into teeny-weeny ceramic cups. Back in the U.S., I had done the Benihana thing where I'm from and had grown quite fond of drinking sake this way. I thought that slurping this lava-hot substance that resembled a cross between rubbing alcohol and straight butane was the way they did it in Japan.

But on that evening in Cape Town, at the other end of the sushi bar, I noticed several Japanese fishermen taking a break from their work off the coast of Africa. They were drinking sake out of what looked like a wine bottle, except it was labeled with big black Japanese characters on beautiful rice paper. I must have been staring, because with a wave of the hand, one of them summoned me to their corner and offered me a taste.

They poured me a glass. "It's not hot?" I asked, thinking they had forgotten to heat the stuff. One of the older fellows said, "First try," pointing to my cup of hot sake. I took a sip of the familiar. Then he motioned for me to try the glass of chilled sake that they had poured. Before I could comment, the older man laughed and said, "Same!" Granted, they weren't the same sakes, but his point was that they were both made of rice and water, and his tasted vastly superior to my hot stuff—like a clean, cool river of flavor gushing through my mouth. In that instant I realized that nothing would be the "same" again. I was both dumbfounded and delighted. I didn't realize it at the moment, but that one little sip of *ginjo* sake would change the course of my life forever.

So, what, since that fateful night in Cape Town, has continued to draw a guy from Ohio to this 1,000-year-old beverage that makes its true home in Japan? This entire book is the long answer to that question. The short answer is that as the owner of True Sake, the first retail store in the world dedicated solely to sake—Japan included—located in San Francisco, California, and as someone who has acquired two professional tasting licenses and a master sake sommelier license (*kikisake-shi*), I can confidently say that sake is one of the most exciting beverages in the world.

Part of this is due to sake's long and varied history. Like most fermented beverages, this deceptively simple but magical combination of rice and water started out crudely and over the years became more and more refined. In Japan, a country where rice has long been an integral part of the country's identity—both symbolically and practically—sake has been at the center of rituals as well as social life. But remarkably, this drink that started out in the hands of monks and remained, until World War II, mostly confined to Japan has become a beverage served in today's trendiest restaurants.

Sake might be ancient in years, but in temperament and style, it's incredibly modern. Clean, yet complex, it pairs well with all types of cuisine. It's relatively low in alcohol, and unlike wine, it has no sulfites, the cause of those nasty hangover headaches. It has a third of the acidity of wine and represents the purest form of alcoholic beverage out there. For those who don't want to start out with sake straight, it also makes a good mixer. Bartenders all over now incorporate it into uniquely flavored cocktails.

As sake becomes more universal, I believe that I'm representative of the new sake drinker. Look at my photo in the back of the book, and you will deduce that I am not Japanese. Upon further inspection you will learn that I neither read nor speak Japanese. As I say to my customers, my greatest strengths are these obvious weaknesses. I can relate to those that know nothing about sake because I've been there too.

The customers who wander into my store full of questions continue to remind me that sake remains an intimidating drink for many. It's understandable. Not only are the labels almost always in Japanese, but there's also a lot of perceived mystery shrouding this libation. Are you supposed to drink it hot or cold? Is there proper etiquette that goes along with it? Even experienced sake drinkers still get stumped by the categories that sake is broken down into, including *junmai*, *ginjo*, and *dai ginjo* (these are all mostly based on how much the rice is polished, but we'll get into that in chapter 4).

On the flip side, experiencing something outside of your own culture liberates you from social mores. Many things that the average *gaijin* (non-Japanese person) sake consumer has encountered—sake cocktails, pairing sake with Western-style meals, serving sake with sushi—have long been no-no's in traditional Japanese sake etiquette. But these new spins on sake are also refreshing and completely unique. Thus you will soon see that a Westerner's "incorrectness" in terms of the confines of sake tradition can actually be a blessing, offering a new sense of appreciation for an ancient beverage.

SITTING IN A SMALL TASTING room in a sake brewery outside of Osaka, Japan, I once asked the ninth-generation president of the brewery why sake made its presence on this great earth. My question, I thought, was both philosophical and curious enough in nature to elicit a profound response. After staring at me for several moments with a thoughtful, but slightly pained, expression on his face, he looked deeply into my eyes and replied, "To have fun."

I hope that through dispelling some of the myths about sake and by telling its story all the way through history to how it's made today, this book will be able to allow you to set aside any hesitations and to have a good time with sake. Along with my coauthor Sara Deseran, we will explore how to pair sake with food and how to make cocktails that highlight sake's nuances (instead of drowning them in hard alcohol), and we will assist you in discovering the sakes that speak to you. Enjoy, and *kanpai* (empty cup)!

—Beau Timken

CHAPTER ONE

THE HISTORY OF SAKE IN JAPAN

ALTHOUGH SAKE ACTUALLY CAME from mainland China, where the first brewing efforts date back to 4800 BC, for the sake of brevity, let's start with Japan, the country that to this day considers sake its national beverage. And as sake is made up of rice and water, let's pick the period in Japan's history when the Japanese started cultivating rice in a wet environment, which was a little more than 2,500 years ago.

13

No one can seem to agree on how exactly sake was first made. Was it discovered when some farmer accidentally let a batch of stored rice go moldy, which then fermented with airborne yeasts? Or was it when some villager employed the decidedly rustic chew-and-spit technique, using the mouth's natural enzymes to break down the starch before fermenting the gruel? What we do know is that the earliest efforts produced a very low-alcohol substance that best resembled your breakfast oatmeal, a gruel that was consumed more for nutritional value than for a buzz. Rather than drink it, people ate it with chopstick-like pincers. But the value of the intoxicating effect was not lost upon the Imperial Court. In AD 689, the Imperial Palace established a brewing department, a movement that took sake from being a common farmer's brew to something that was valued by the rulers of society.

At some point in the next 100 years, most likely with the help of the Chinese, sake production became more efficient. A new technique was established that used a mold to break down the rice, rather than the chew-and-spit system. During this time, it was also established that sake should be made to please the Shinto gods. The gods and sake were joined at the hip, and at any religious event, sake was an essential component—enough so that monks at individual temples and shrines became the first formal brewers outside of the Imperial Court.

SAKE BECOMES BIG BUSINESS

Arguably, the Japanese have long been perfectionists. Sake was no exception. Over the next 400 years, sake was fine-tuned and ultimately started being made using methods that are still honored today. By the sixteenth century, local breweries, run by brewers who catered to the common man, took over the market from the monks who had been serving the more aristocratic and wealthy circles. Now, different styles of sake started to take form, each influenced by the areas where they were produced, reflecting both the landscape and the predominant cuisine. Some areas grew better rice, some areas had superior water, and some areas had better climates for peak production conditions. Kyoto and Kobe became recognized as the premier brewing centers for many of these reasons.

Around 1575, two major developments occurred that would change sake forever. First, rice started being polished, which meant sake was now being made from white rice, while it had previously been made from brown. Gone were the fats, proteins, vitamins, minerals, and other impurities that were responsible for the off-flavors in sake. Around this time, the elaborate and exacting Japanese tea ceremony brought sake into the social and cultural folds, and for the first time, food and sake were married.

By 1698, more than 27,000 sake breweries dotted the island of Japan. Sake represented the spirit and community of every inch of Japan. Small local breweries constructed sakes to be paired with the local cuisine. If a brewery was located close to the ocean, it made sake that went well with seafood, and if a brewery was in the mountains, its sake was likely to complement meats and mountain vegetables. The incorporation of waterwheel mills and massive fermentation tanks, the use of distilled alcohol to preserve batches, faster brewing techniques, and better transportation dramatically aided the massive increases in sake production. Seeing the lucrative side of sake, the government eventually got involved, a liquor tax was implemented, and home brewing of sake was banned.

In the 1800s, both mass producers and small microbrewers (who made what's called *jizake*, or "local sake") defined the industry. While major brewing centers in Kobe and Kyoto were brewing sake for national distribution, numerous local breweries started catering to narrower regional markets, turning out sakes with regional flavors and styles that reflected the different water and rice used for brewing. For example, areas with harder water produced bigger-flavored sakes, while prefectures with softer water made lighter brews. The style of Kobe sake came to be known as masculine and less fragrant than sake from Kyoto, which was known for its feminine, light, and aromatic qualities. Niigata sake was considered pristine, Okayama sake was sweeter than most, and Hiroshima produced a very soft and light product.

Now one could taste brews from different parts of the country. But within individual communities, all of this competition actually created an extreme sense of loyalty to the local brew, a loyalty that still exists today for much of the older generation. Today, for the most part, only younger sake consumers venture to purchase sakes from outside their region.

JAPAN'S NEW IDENTITY

There are many cultural parallels between the history of sake in Japan and wine in France and beer in Germany. But although each beverage has played a part in unifying *and* regionalizing its country, making bedmates of religion and alcohol, and promoting an identity that people use to define themselves, Japan's relationship with sake was deeper. By the mid-1800s, Japan had acquired a new identity: sake *was* Japan and vice versa.

Both geographically and culturally, the country was essentially isolated, with little outside influence. Despite the fact that the origins of sake may have come from abroad, the Japanese claimed sake as their own; there really were no other alcoholic beverages. Couple this with the facts that symbolically rice was everything to the Japanese—it was even used as currency at one point—and that sake *is* essentially made of only rice, and you can start to see how sake came to represent the essence of all things Japanese.

In 1904, the government did a surprising thing, something that supported this relatively new identity. Despite its pervasive history of taxes and manipulation of the sake industry, the ruling party shifted the government's position on sake and decided to take an active role in the future of the "drink of the gods." It opened the National Research Institute of Brewing to promote changes in the sake field. It was quite a novel concept, and it has few, if any, equals throughout the history of alcoholic beverages around the world. (Imagine the U.S. government promoting the betterment of beer!)

Among other activities, the National Research Institute of Brewing cosponsored a nationwide competition that pitted breweries from all over Japan against each other to see who could make the best sake in the land. The national sake competition changed sake forever. This competition became the be-all and end-all for the reputations of breweries. It also promoted and regulated the grading, classification, and categorization of sakes.

So how was all of this sake being consumed? With a vengeance. Sake had become a drink for almost everyone. For the man on the street who couldn't afford an inn or a teahouse in which to imbibe, there were small drinking huts called *izakaya*, which could be anything from a one-room shop to four poles holding up a canvas roof. For those who couldn't afford finer food, the *sakana*, or sake food, was often made of small portions of miso paste, red pepper, or salt. (If you have ever been served a little pinch of salt on your cedar box of sake in a restaurant, this hearkens back to these early days.) Of course sake was still used in religious ceremonies, but it was also now accepted socially and Japanese drinkers were starting to have some serious fun—up until the conflict with China and World War II.

FORTIFIED SAKE

The ugliness of war had a direct influence on the sake industry. Japanese soldiers were starving abroad, and the citizens back home felt the tight grip of governmental rationing of rice. All rice went into consumption. There was neither time, nor rice, for sake. As a result, breweries closed left and right, and at one point only 3,000 breweries remained.

But soon it was discovered that if cheap distilled alcohol was blended with sake, a new kind of sake could be made using very little rice. And that is exactly what happened. Sake was made using distilled grain alcohol, sugars, and rice extracts to expand batch yields. (Even a synthetic sake was produced, using no rice whatsoever.) In terms of taste, sake grew talons, becoming quite potent and harsh. An entire generation of sake drinkers got used to this flavor profile, and as a result, many older Japanese to this day prefer the taste of big and boozy sakes and frown upon the lighter-tasting sakes that became the trend after the war.

Nevertheless, the genie was out of the bottle, and the addition of distilled alcohol became a regulated and integral part of sake in Japan. The use of added alcohol in sake today has become an accepted norm to enhance aroma, flavor, and texture, although some purists still turn up their noses at it.

MODERN-DAY JAPAN

Ironically, after World War II the same society that had previously prided itself on its individuality began to crave all things that were not Japanese—and alcoholic beverages were no exception. There was a massive rush to consume whiskey, beer, and European wines, and by the 1980s the once proud and dominant fermented rice beverage represented only 15 percent of the entire alcohol market in Japan. New drinkers raced to Western-style beverages, discarding sake as their father's drink.

Today, while sake has become trendy and appealing to a new generation of foreign consumers around the globe, brewers have tried to woo younger Japanese back to the drink by making sweeter sakes, sparkling sake, and lower-alcohol products focusing a great deal on packaging. The current movement is to produce sakes that are more "winelike" to lure the wine drinkers both in Japan and abroad.

THE NEW ARTISANAL SAKE

But there's been a positive side to this change. Although the market for table sake is decreasing at an alarming rate, production of premium and artisanal sakes continues to go in the other direction, a movement that started in the '70s when small breweries started brewing expressive, complex, and fragrant yeast-driven sakes.

Before this time, breweries reserved their "special effort" sake only for the national sake competition, but that all changed when a few brewers decided to brew their amazing competition-only sake all the time. The decision to make competition sake year-round gave birth to the new *ginjo*, or premium sake, a movement that we are reaping the benefits of today.

CHAPTER TWO

SAKE GOES GLOBAL

WHILE SAKE IS GLOBALLY regarded as a Japanese beverage, it has long been consumed in other Asian countries such as Korea and China in various fermented and distilled forms. But the United States was sake's first real stop abroad. As reported in the *Honolulu Advertiser*, sake made its way to what would become U.S. shores in 1885 when Japanese immigrants working on the sugar plantations brought sake to Hawaii.

19

These immigrants imported so much sake that the Japanese government created a duty tax of 600 percent on sake to discourage more people from leaving Japan. By the early 1900s, roughly fifteen sake breweries existed in the United States. Although they disappeared quickly, sake had touched the United States, and this eventually led to the country's unique history of brewing Japan's national beverage outside of Japan. Since then, places such as Australia and South America have made efforts to brew their own sake, but to this day, no other Western country has embraced the production of sake quite like the United States.

It took until the 1970s for sake to find its way back to the West in a production capacity. Several major Japanese breweries in Japan (Ozeki, Shochikubai, Gekkeikan, and Harushika) settled on the West Coast of the United States to produce domestic

sake for a market that they felt would soon increase in demand. They also hoped to ship this foreign-made sake back to Japan in an attempt to undercut a brutal price war on cheap, low-end sake.

In terms of exporting sake to the West, specifically to the United States in the late '70s, Japanese breweries didn't see the reason to share their better sakes. They relied upon food companies to act as the importers and ambassadors for sake representation abroad. Sadly, these companies considered sake as an afterthought and sold it as a side note; it traveled in nonrefrigerated shipping containers with foodstuffs and chopsticks. There was little education about proper handling and serving methods; thus, for those drinkers who didn't know better, it became popular to heat sake to the point of not being able to taste the inferiority of the product. For most, sake was still a novel Japanese beverage that was served piping hot at sushi bars—a very rough version, as most of the product that restaurants were pushing was old and damaged. To the Japanese exporters, the overseas markets represented a dumping ground for the sake that they themselves didn't want.

To this day, most people take their first sip of sake at a sushi bar. Indeed, the history of sake abroad owes its past—and future—to sushi's popularity. Luckily, by the time the 1990s rolled around, the good stuff had come out from under the sushi counter, and premium sakes were, and increasingly are, enjoyed by people all over the world.

There's a long way to go, but the future looks good. Sake landed abroad without much of an instruction manual, but slowly and surely Westerners are finding their sake legs, if you will. Enterprising sake-only importers started the trend of sake promotion and were aided by two Western writers living in Japan, Philip Harper and John Gauntner, who crafted books to guide us through the experience of sake. Now a new movement, led by adventurous bartenders who create sake cocktails, has pushed the boundaries of sake in a whimsical way. Equally daring chefs are breaking down the myth that sake must be served only with Japanese food. Pairing sake with Western cuisine represents the future of the beverage outside of Japan.

Another sign that things have changed is that sake, once available only at Japanese grocery stores, can now be found in major chain food stores. Wine shops have also jumped into the game, offering limited selections of the "wine of Japan," and four-star restaurants that have little to do with Asian food have incorporated high-end sakes into their bar selections.

There is no denying that sake has become a global beverage. Many of the current president/owners of Japanese breweries have lived and been educated overseas, and they have a vastly different outlook on the world than their parents had. As the world at large embraces sake, Japanese brewers have started to examine the taste profiles of Americans, other Asians, and Europeans to better gauge what types of sake to brew. Interestingly, in the twenty-first century, the global market potentially represents the future for this incredible drink that used to define an ancient and noble Japanese society.

Sake Lingo 101

Headed to Japan or a party full of sake geeks? Here are some basic "need to know" sake terms that will come in handy and make you sound like a pro.

nihonshu The unofficial term for sake in Japan. The word *sake* actually refers to all types of alcoholic beverages, from wine and beer to mixed drinks.

seishu The legal word for filtered or clear sake; you'll see it printed on most bottles, but few people use it in conversation.

tokubetsu A special *junmai* made with a higher than normal polishing rate.

kanpai The most popular sake-drinking toast, which translates as "empty cup."

kura or **sakagura** A sake brewery.

kurabito The people who work in a brewery.

toji The head brewer.

amakuchi A sweeter sake.

karakuchi A drier sake.

atsukan Hot sake.

hiya-zake Cold sake.

masu The cedar box that was originally used for measuring rice and is often used for drinking sake.

choko or **o-choko** The small ceramic cups used to drink sake.

sakaya A store that sells sake.

jizake Local sake or product from a small and traditional sake brewery (comparable to a beer microbrewery).

izakaya A small restaurant that specializes in sake and foods that go best with sake.

yake-zake Drinking to get drunk.

CHAPTER THREE

SAKE RITUALS

Drinking sake has always been part of a way of life in both the ancient and modern cultures of Japan, from emperors using sake to reward their court to families sharing a taste with the gods on New Year's Day. The role of sake in the religious context dates back to 200 BC when farmers would pray for better harvests, anointing the crops with sake and drinking it as part of the ceremony.

Later, in a more formalized religious capacity, monks not only brewed sake, but they also made it a part of most everything that called for worship. Sake was seen as a way to get closer to the deities, and events were not complete without a cup being filled for those beyond this world. Even today, in the thousands of little roadside shrines that dot the Japanese countryside, you will see a filled sake cup among the other objects of prayer.

From births and weddings to war and death, sake has long been a part of uniting people in a way that spoken words cannot. A perfect example is the typical Japanese Shinto wedding, which to this day calls for the bride and groom to partake in the consumption of sake in a formal ritual. *San-san kudo* is the act in which a cup of sake is passed back and forth three times between the bride and groom to consecrate their wedding vows during the formal ceremony. But sake's role at a wedding is not over with that. At the reception, the newlyweds are presented with an enormous cask filled with sake, and they jointly break open the top of the cask in a ritual very much like cutting the wedding cake.

Like Champagne, sake is often presented as a gift of good luck and blessing for momentous occasions: the birth of a baby, a promotion at work, graduations, and housewarmings. If, for example, you were to break ground on a new home or office building, a priest would be summoned to sprinkle sake on the earth to rid the site of evil spirits and to bless the grounds. Likewise, in the sports world, a cask of sake is buried under sumo wrestling platforms to purify the ring. And when a sumo champion is crowned, he is always presented with an enormous bowl of sake to be consumed in one swig. Even at the conclusion of major Formula One car racing events, the winners shake and spray bottles of sparkling sake rather than Champagne.

While sake is used for joyous events, it's an integral part of funerals and is used to bless the departed and to give comfort to the family and friends of the deceased. During World War II, this took on new meaning when Japanese kamikaze pilots drank sake before boarding their planes, which were used as missiles against their enemies.

When sake was first introduced in a nonreligious capacity, it was as an accompaniment to the fastidious Japanese tea ceremony. The highly orchestrated ritual espoused the simple aspects of life and was preceded by an elaborate, yet starkly simple, meal called *kaiseki*, which featured an array of small, meticulously arranged portions of food. During the ceremony, three cups of sake would be offered in a succinct and calculated fashion. Each movement was calculated, from cup placement to how one drank the sake.

One sake tradition that endures today is an offshoot from the ritualistic tea ceremony. Called *o-shaku*, it's the concept of pouring sake for your companion, who in return pours for you. This tradition's original purpose was meant to garner an instant relationship with another person. Today, though, if two friends are close, it is not considered necessary to pour for the other. Also, the more modern use of larger glasses has slightly diminished its role. Should someone tell you that it's bad luck to drink from a cup that you yourself poured, be comforted that this is merely a popular myth.

Although many of the formalities brought about by the tea ceremony lived on for years, the lines of sake etiquette shifted in the 1970s and '80s when sake's role went from its use in sedate social occasions to being an accepted, almost mandatory, social lubricant for Japanese businessmen, who headed straight from work to bars around town. (Soon, sake was even being sold in coin-operated dispensing machines in lobbies and train stations.) Today, working women have joined this tradition, and you'll often see officemates packing into small bars that are void of chairs and instead offer counters to accommodate the women and their beverages of choice. In fact, when a business deal is consummated, it's rarely done in the office, but rather at a karaoke bar, where people pour sake for one another as an act of respect.

CHAPTER FOUR

HOW RICE AND WATER MAKE SAKE

IF SAKE-MAKING IS A GRAND PRODUCTION, then the lead actor—the one who holds the entire performance together—would most definitely be rice. Beyond its cultural significance, rice, as a grain, is far more complex than one might imagine. In nature, white rice doesn't exist. Any white rice that you have consumed is actually brown rice that has been polished (milled) to a certain extent, typically between 10 and 12 percent, with 90 percent of the white grain remaining.

Sake rice, on the other hand, is far starchier than edible rice. (Remember, sake-makers are looking for starch content, not nutrients.) A grain of sake rice is also larger than table rice and much hardier. It has to be able to stand up to the friction and heat created in the milling process. Thus, the most desirable brewing rice is hard on the outside and soft on the inside.

Just like grapes for wine-making, there are many different kinds of rice for sake-making. Currently, there are roughly sixty varieties of brewing rice commonly used. The most famous is called Yamada Nishiki, a rice that is so popular in the brewing world that there is a movement to break down the national sake competition into two classes: sakes with Yamada Nishiki and those without. Yamada Nishiki comes from a brewing rice called Omachi, the granddaddy of many of the currently used varietals. But not every brewery uses it. Each selects a rice that works best with the available water and for the type of sake that the brewery wants to produce.

IT'S IN THE WATER

While rice is indeed important, sake is made up of at least 80 percent water, so one could just as easily argue that the water used in brewing sake is the most important ingredient. If a brewery's water is not good, then the rice quality doesn't mean as much.

For a while in history, water wasn't considered to be a crucial element. But brewers began noticing that sakes made in different locations using rice milled to the same levels and the same techniques had very different flavors. Some water just works better with some rice. Areas such as Kobe and Kyoto became the brewing capitals because they had the most suitable water. What makes good sake-making water? Potassium, magnesium, and phosphoric acid help rice to do its thing, whereas iron does just the opposite. Also, whether water is hard or soft gives a sake unique qualities as well.

THE MAGIC OF YEAST

How can something made only of rice and water—both almost blank slates, in terms of flavor—end up tasting like everything from melons and green apples to ripe strawberries, chestnuts, and honeysuckle? The first of many answers would be yeast.

Yeasts are all around us at all times, up on your rafter and nesting in your carpet. The brewing industry discovered over time that these yeasts could be captured and cultivated by taking the foam that's produced in sake-making (the foam is caused by the sugars being converted to alcohol and carbon dioxide), drying it, and voilà! Breweries began to create their own proprietary yeasts this way, which resulted in different flavors and forms of sake.

These yeasts then were mass-produced by the Japan Sake Brewer's Association, which collected and sold them to all sake-makers. Of course, some breweries will never sell the secret concoctions that help distinguish their sake, but on the whole it is the industry standard for breweries to buy yeasts. These are numbered from one to seventeen and are referred to as Association No. 7 or Association No. 9, each distinct in its aroma, flavors, and other properties. Many of the brewing regions also have their own prefecture, or regional, yeasts, such as Shizouka No. 2 and Yamagata No. 1.

THE PROCESS OF MAKING SAKE

Considering there is no end to the methods used to make sake, the best way to explain the brewing process is to focus on the general concepts. It is up to you to go to Japan and visit a brewery to learn its specific technique.

POLISHING THE RICE

The first step is to polish or mill sake-brewing rice. Polishing is a function of removing the outer layers of rice, which include the fats, proteins, minerals, and vitamins, to reach a more abundant layer of starch. This is done in large machines that have vertical pivoted rollers that scrape away layer after layer. A percentage is calculated by the weight of the removed shavings for each grain of rice. For example, rice that is milled to 60 percent means that 40 percent of each and every grain has been removed.

These numbers are important, since they represent the way that sake is categorized. Sake is not categorized by rice varieties, as wine is categorized by grapes such as Chardonnay and Cabernet; rather, the sake industry uses polishing rates to define the purity level of each type of sake. Rice that has been milled to 70 percent has more of the outside of each grain of rice than does rice that has been polished to 50 percent; thus, the rice with a 50 percent milling ratio is considered to be the purer of the two. It is a general rule that the more the rice is milled, the more expensive the sake, as it is more labor intensive and requires longer and more costly milling time. Typically, sake rice that is polished to 50 percent will require forty to fifty hours in the milling machine. There are several premium sakes that are polished to 28 percent, meaning 72 percent of each grain is removed. Such rice is on the milling machine for seventy-two hours or more.

These long hours heat up and dry out the rice, and it is imperative to allow freshly polished rice of all milling rates to sit for fourteen to twenty days to cool. Although every brewery does it differently, the goal is for the rice to stabilize with a little humidity filling out the grains. For example, one brewery might place wet towels over the bags of milled rice, while another brewery puts the polished rice in mesh bags for greater air and humidity exposure. One brewery I know of actually keeps the milled rice in a room with an air filter so as to keep air pollution from infecting the delicately polished rice.

WASHING, SOAKING, AND STEAMING THE RICE

The second step is to wash the polished rice. This step is needed to remove the last of the "dirty" elements, including any sugars that may remain on the newly uncovered outside layer. The washed rice is then soaked in fresh water. The goal is to get water into the center of each grain of rice. The more water a grain of rice contains, the easier it is to steam, which accelerates the conversion from starch to glucose, or sugar.

Steaming the rice is next and is crucial for two main reasons: the heat explodes starch granules in the rice, which then helps the *koji* mold do its job of breaking the starch down evenly and effectively, and the heat also sterilizes the rice. Many breweries still use the more labor-intensive manual steaming technique, while other breweries use machines that steam the rice on a conveyor belt of sorts.

Now you have hot rice that needs to be cooled down before the next vital step. Typically, this is done in one of two ways. The old-world method is to spread the rice out on large cotton tarps on the floor of the brewery to allow the rice to cool. The new method calls for a machine that is part comb, cool-air blower, and conveyor belt. The fingers of the comb break up the clumps, and the cool air gets blown onto the hot rice.

KOJI: THE SECRET WEAPON

Now it's time to introduce the *koji*, the mold that helps break up the starch to allow it to become glucose. Just what does *koji* look like? It's a yellowish greenish powder that looks almost like a spice. Though brewers may dispute which of the other steps is the most important, more brewers claim that the excellence of the final product depends on the effectiveness and quality of the *koji*.

Koji has three main roles: to help break down the starch into sugar, to induce yeast to breed, and eventually to give the sake's flavor some character and style. To prepare to incorporate the *koji*, brewers spread out the rice on a long table. When the rice has been matted down by hand, they sprinkle the *koji* mold on the rice as evenly as possible. Then hands—lots of hands—start massaging the nearly invisible *koji* powder into the rice. At this point, the rice is called the *koji*, as it is carrying the mold spores within it.

Steamed rice is the perfect environment for mold. It is wet and warm, and it has lots for a mold to eat. The mold on the *koji* rice germinates within hours, as brewers keep the *koji* rooms as warm and humid as possible. (Think of your shower floor.) Mold grows like mad; within forty-eight hours, the batch is usually fully "living." The difficult part is keeping the temperature perfect for the mold to grow but not die. And, of course, some maintain the *koji* the old-fashioned way, mixing and stirring the flattened rice by hand twice every four hours, while some use a machine to rotate the trays filled with *koji* automatically. It takes a lifetime to truly understand how to make good *koji*, and that is why this step is often referred to as the first step in the sake-making process.

MOTO: THE YEAST STARTER

The next step is designed to fire up yeast cells in a concentrated liquid concoction called the *moto*, or yeast starter. It is made from *koji* rice, steamed rice, pure yeast cells, and lactic acid, and it produces a small but effective amount of highly concentrated, yeast-filled fluid that is used to expand the rest of the batch of sake, if you will. It is a safe house for the yeasts, which go wild.

There have been many different ways to achieve this yeast starter, from the *kimoto* method, which calls for ramming the mixture with wooden poles, to the *yamahai* method, which allows airborne yeasts to join the party naturally. Either way, the end result is a superconcentrated starter liquid that greatly helps the next fermenting stage.

MOROMI: THE MAIN MASH

At this point, you're probably wondering when the fermenting takes place. Well, the wait is over, as now it's time for the *moromi*, or the main mash. Staying true to the complexity of making sake, this step is actually broken down into three parts called the "mixing in three stages" or "three-step brewing" process. But, first, a visual: Imagine a huge vat, the largest soup can in the world, perhaps. Now recall the previously prepared elements—the steamed rice, the *koji* rice, the yeast starter. The mash is a mix of all of these elements in that vat. But it's not as simple as adding everything at once. In fact, you add the elements in three successions in four days (with day two being a day of rest).

Now we have a huge vat filled with all of these tediously prepared elements that will ferment for the next fifteen to eighteen days. But remember one important fact during this fermenting process: fermentation is being accompanied by saccharification at the same time. During this period of activity, the brewers can control the final product in terms of sweet versus dry, thick versus thin, rich versus light, and so on, all by adding the different prepared elements in different quantities and at different temperatures. At the end of the fermentation cycle, brewers have the option to add a little distilled alcohol if they intend on making a certain category of sake, but of course this addition kills off the remaining working yeasts and stops fermentation completely.

There is nothing like walking through a room full of vats filled with fermenting sake. The active ingredients are truly active. As the conversion takes place, large bubbles dance in the foam. Sometimes a brewer proclaims a batch finished simply by regarding the size and active popping of the bubbles in the foam.

PRESSING AND FILTERING THE SAKE

Now any solid parts of the rice that remain are separated by pressing the mixture. This, too, is done either the old way or the new way. The older method is to fill cotton bags with the fermented sake and place them side by side in a box, like sardines in a tin. Then a lid is placed on the box, which is tightened shut, and the sake fluid runs out a spout in the bottom of the box. Today, however, more brewers use a large machine that looks a lot like an accordion. There is also a luxurious type of pressing called *shizuku*, which calls for the cotton bags of rice mash to be hung in the air, allowing gravity to slowly press the mash against the sacks.

The next step is a bit confusing, as it is called filtering, and there exists something called unfiltered sake, which is sake with some of the lees produced by the mash left in the fluid. Despite that, in this case, filtering means running the liquid through a machine, where it is introduced to charcoal, which strips out any unwanted flavors, colors, or elements—not unlike a water filter. However, there is a movement in the industry to stop filtering so much and to allow sake to retain its true color and feeling.

PASTEURIZATION

The last step is pasteurization. This can be done with already bottled sake or by running sake through a pipe that is submerged in superheated water. The goal is to reach a temperature of about 150 degrees Fahrenheit. Every brewery has a different approach, and this includes the number of times the sake is heated and when it is done. Typically, brewers fire the sake twice: once before storing it, and once before they ship it. Brewers can also choose to add water at this time to bring the alcohol level back to 14 to 15 percent from its peak of about 20 percent, but some don't. Likewise, some brewers may also make the call not to pasteurize at all.

Sake Categories

IF THE PROCESS of sake-making wasn't complex enough, the way in which sake is categorized can make matters more confusing. Sake is not categorized by rice varieties. Rather, it is first categorized by milling rates of polished brewing rice and then further classified by the ingredients of the sake under names such as *junmai* and *honjozo*. These concepts and words take some getting used to. But take a deep breath and read on. With a little thought, it's not as complicated as it looks.

The most important thing to remember is if the sake is made of just rice and water, it is distinguished by the term *junmai*. Sake brewers also add a bit of distilled alcohol to some types of sake to bring out different flavors, aromas, and textures, and this creates a new category called *honjozo* for these alcohol-added sakes. But to confuse you a bit more, the term *junmai* also historically means sake that has been milled at least 30 percent with 70 percent of each grain remaining, but new guidelines stipulate that sake may still be called a *junmai* even if the milling rate is below the industry standard of 30 percent and only if this percentage is made clear on the label.

Junmai is a sake that is made of rice and water with grains of rice that have been polished at least 30 percent with 70 percent of the grain remaining.

Junmai ginjo is a sake that is made of rice and water with grains of rice that have been polished at least 40 percent with 60 percent of the grain remaining.

Junmai dai ginjo is a sake that is made of rice and water with grains of rice that have been polished at least 50 percent with 50 percent of the grain remaining.

Honjozo is a sake that is made with distilled alcohol and grains of rice that have been polished at least 30 percent with 70 percent of the grain remaining.

Ginjo is a sake that is made with distilled alcohol with grains of rice that have been polished at least 40 percent with 60 percent of the grain remaining.

Dai ginjo is a sake that is made with distilled alcohol and grains of rice that have been polished at least 50 percent with 50 percent of the grain remaining.

OTHER TYPES OF SAKE

Nigori is a sake that has been purposely left unfiltered and has the lees or rice polishings left in the bottle. Typically, the sake looks foggy or cloudy.

Genshu is a sake that has been purposely left undiluted with no extra water added to bring the alcohol level down from its natural fermentation percentage of between 18 and 20 percent. Sake typically has an alcohol content between 14 and 16 percent.

Nama is a sake that has been purposely left unpasteurized and is referred to as "living" sake. Sake is usually pasteurized twice.

The Trick to Reading a Sake Label

TO A WESTERNER who doesn't read *kanji*, or Japanese characters, a sake label can be beautiful but intimidating. Never fear: just look for the numbers. First, there is almost always a polishing rate hidden among the characters. For example, if you see "60%," you will know that it's a ginjo; if you see "45%," you'll know that it's a dai ginjo. You may also see a +4 or a –1, the sake meter value (see page 52). There is also a chance that you'll see acidity and amino acid levels around 1.4 or 1.8 for acidity and 1.3 or 1.2 for the amino acids. If the acidity is high—as in 1.8 or higher—the sake could very well be a genshu, or a *yamahai* or *kimoto* method, both old-style sakes, which are full-bodied. Of course, you will also recognize the alcohol percentage, which is usually around 15 to 16 percent. And if you look closely you will sometimes notice a date. Obviously, 03.09 would mean a bottling date of September 2003. But what does 16.03 mean? This is based on the emperor's calendar, and it starts when a new emperor takes the throne. As it so happens, that last change of emperors occurred in 1988, which makes 2006 the number 18. So if you read 14.02 on a label, that means the sake was bottled in February 2002 and is probably spoiled or out of date and shouldn't be purchased.

Although labels are hardly consistent in their layout, they are becoming more accessible. People such as myself have been pushing importers to add more English to the back labels of sake to provide simple information such as the translated name of the sake, where it was made, its classification, and a brief description of the style of sake from a brewer's perspective. Still, the best way to remember the sakes you like is to write down the name and a brief physical description of the label for future use.

純米大吟醸「古典寫樂」

アルコール分	15度以上16度未満
日本酒度	(+) 3
酸度	1.3
使用酵母	協会9号
好適米銘柄	美山錦
精米歩合	50%
醪最高温度	10度
杜氏氏名	会津杜氏 渡部喜代美
製造年月	16. 12. --

清酒

原材料名 米、米麹

東山酒造合資会社

電話 0242－22－1242

※飲酒は20歳になってから。

CHAPTER FIVE

TASTING, SELECTING, AND SERVING SAKE

WHEN IT COMES TO SAKE TASTING, there is really no right or wrong. As Hiroshi Kondo, the first Japanese sake guru to write a book in English, once wrote, "Drinking is a human sport, and lurking within all sake connoisseurship are broad areas of subjective appraisal." Certainly, another person can recommend a sake he or she thinks you might like, but ultimately it's important to gain enough confidence to realize that only *you* know what tastes good to you.

37

TIME, PLACE, AND OCCASION

Just like there are no two identical snowflakes, there are no two identical palates. The chemical makeup of each person's mouth is completely unique and the mind-body experience can't be ignored. Emotions such as anger, excitement, joy, and sadness all play a part as to how something tastes. Along with some other folks, I've come to call this phenomenon TPO—or time, place, and occasion—and it is quite an important concept in sake tasting.

IDENTIFYING AROMA AND TASTE

Despite the fact that sake tasting is very personal, the human desire to quantify it is age-old. There are 600 documented aroma components and almost twice as many flavor components that have been used to describe sake. Of course, all it takes is a person to say, "This sake smells like Velveeta" to create a new, generally accepted aroma. Professionally trained individuals spend countless hours trying to dissect sake so that others can get a sense of what to expect.

Tools have been developed over the years to help this process. One such tool is known as the quadrants of sake, which breaks sake down into the following categories:

1. fragrant
2. light and smooth
3. rich
4. aged or mature

There's also the old Japanese concept of the five flavors that need to be in perfect balance:

1. sweet
2. dry
3. bitter
4. sour/acidic
5. astringent

Considering all of these variables, it's a good thing to learn how to break down exactly what *you* prefer about one sake or another. Of course, professional sake tasters, who taste up to 120 sakes at a time, know what they're looking for before they even start out. To help you discover elements of sake that best suit you, here's a checklist for tasting sake that's very helpful.

LISTEN

This may sound odd, but try listening to the bottle being opened, the sound of sake being poured, and the sound of the fluid sloshing around a glass or a cup. Taking in all of this makes sake drinking even more pleasurable.

LOOK

Don't forget to look before you leap. Your eyes can tell you more than you might imagine. Despite the fact that in Japan the traditional tasting cup is white ceramic

NISHINOSEKI *"Champion of the West"*

Junmai; Oita Prefecture; SMV: -3; Acidity: 1.5. With a
nose of sweet flowers hidden among mushrooms, nuts,
and cream, the first sip of this junmai is like tasting a
sip of buttery popcorn. Don't let the low SMV fool you,
as this guy drinks more savory than sweet. Champion of
the West is probably one of the softest sakes in the biz,
despite its deep and expansive flavors. This shimmering
junmai is great chilled and even better warmed up.

WORD:	Creamy
WINE:	Soft reds, creamy whites
BEER:	Ales
FOOD:	Take-out Chinese, fried chicken, tempura.

NIWA NO UGUISU *"Daruma"*

Tokubetsu Junmai; Fukuoka Prefecture; SMV: +4; Acidity:
1.4. Daruma has a brilliant collection of aromas from
cinnamon and steamed vegetables to celery and grains.
It has a soft, smoky start that is chewy and filled with
ripe fruit tones but without the sweetness. This is a big-
flavored sake that has licks of rice, grains, and honey.
It drinks very silky and watery smooth. There's a clean
delivery of flavor from front to back with a very veiled
anisette twinge.

WORD:	Silky
WINE:	Vivid reds, thick whites
BEER:	Big ales, soft stouts
FOOD:	Smoky dishes. A hit with spaghetti Bolognese.

OTOKOYAMA *"Man's Mountain"*

Junmai Dai Ginjo; Hokkaido Prefecture; SMV: +5; Acidity:
1.3. Welcome to one of the preeminent dai ginjos in the
history of premium sakes—a special sake for a special
occasion. The elegant nose is filled with sweet rice, white
chocolate, and juicy pineapple. A silky walk of plum skin
and straw flavors fills the mouth with a velvety push
that quickly ends. At each level, you'll discover flavors
such as pomegranate, minerals, and sweet potatoes, all
of the elements working in harmony to create more than
just a sip of sake; it's a taste of history itself.

WORD:	Elegant
WINE:	Dry reds, Sauvignon Blancs
BEER:	Fresh ales
FOOD:	Haute cuisine. Think delicate and poached, such as seafood terrine.

OTOKOYAMA UTAMARO *"Famous Painter"*

Tokubetsu Junmai; Hokkaido Prefecture; SMV: +2; Acidity: 1.5. Famous Painter is a great example of a sake that drinks like it smells. A floral aroma with touches of bananas, papaya, and cream is mirrored by flavors of tropical fruits, cashews, and whipping cream. With a subtle acidity, this junmai is both complex and refreshingly simple, a good representation of a "layered" sake with elements that work on different planes.

WORD:	Layered
WINE:	Rosés, dry Chardonnays
BEER:	Pale ales, wheat beers
FOOD:	Crab dumplings, cold soba noodles, steamed fish.

OZEKI OSAKAYA CHOBEI *"First Boss"*

Dai Ginjo; Hyogo Prefecture; SMV: +4; Acidity: 1.3. This is a terrific value as it gives a drinker the chance to taste a real player in the history of Japanese sake. The nose is pure strawberry, while the honeydew start is relaxed with a round finish. Look for a middle mouth filled with ripe melon flavors and a sweetness that isn't sweet. (Go figure!) The viscosity is slick, and the mouth speed is velvety and quick. An abundance of ripe flavors cascades down the throat.

WORD:	Honeydew
WINE:	Chewy reds, ripe whites
BEER:	Sweet ales
FOOD:	A guarantee with bacon-wrapped shrimp, but try dim sum and sake-steamed clams.

RIHAKU *"Dreamy Clouds"*

Tokubetsu Junmai Nigori; Shimane Prefecture; SMV: +3; Acidity: 1.6. This nigori is the complete package for those looking for a subtle chewy and creamy sake that has a complex aroma profile and flavor waves of nuts, ripe fruits, toffee, and a tinge of banana. With a pronounced acidity, it has a subtle sweetness but leaves a dry mouth. Soft and supple, it appeals to people that like both sweet and dry.

WORD:	Milky
WINE:	Creamy Chardonnays
BEER:	Ales
FOOD:	Bar snacks, smoked fish, and macaroni and cheese.

SATO NO HOMARE *"Pride of the Village"*

Junmai Ginjo; Ibaraki Prefecture; SMV: +3; Acidity: 1.3.
This sake is sake history itself. Brewed by the oldest
active brewery in Japan, which was founded in 1147,
its current president is a fifty-fifth-generation family
owner. With a refreshingly light nose mixed with
banana, *koji* rice, and cotton candy, it's full of ripe fruit
flavors in a delicious chewy package. Bordering on
syrupy, it drinks surprisingly dry. A very good sake for
those looking to make the leap from expressive wines.

WORD:	History
WINE:	Chardonnays, Pinot Noirs
BEER:	Sweet ales
FOOD:	Elegant dishes of buttery shellfish, fish mousse, and sashimi.

SENPUKU KURA *"Wine Cellar of 1,000 Fortunes"*

Junmai Dai Ginjo; Hiroshima Prefecture; SMV: +3; Acidity: 1.6. This dai ginjo has a nectarine-and-dried-fruit
nose with a slight hint of coconut. Dry for a dai ginjo,
it has a springy start and grassy middle mouth. The viscosity is thick and abundant without overwhelming the
subtle acidity. With lots of character and attitude, it's
definitely a red wine drinker's choice.

WORD:	Robust
WINE:	Big Cabernets, burly Zinfandels
BEER:	Guinness, stouts
FOOD:	Hearty fare such as juicy burgers and breaded chicken.

SHIRAKAWAGO SANSANIGORI *"Bamboo Leaf"*

Junmai Ginjo Nigori; Gifu Prefecture; SMV: +1; Acidity:
1.5. This elegant ginjo nigori is a creamy coconut slide
wrapped in a milky mouth with a great finish that's
fairly clean. With a nose of rose petals and raisins, it has
a smooth texture with a viscosity that's on the thin side.
It definitely appeals to those looking for a semisweet,
slippery nigori, great for blending in cocktails.

WORD:	Coconut
WINE:	Semidry whites
BEER:	Creamy ales
FOOD:	Spicy Asian foods such as coconut curry and chile-laced sushi rolls.

SHIRATAKI JOZEN MIZUNOGOTOSHI
"Pure Flavor"

Junmai Ginjo; Niigata Prefecture; SMV: +3; Acidity: 1.4. With a complex aroma profile filled with minerals, persimmons, and pomegranates, the image that best fits this wonderfully clean ginjo is melting snow on a sunny day. There is a mysterious white chocolate beginning that meets a vanilla middle, culminating in a dried-apple finish. The smoothness and thin viscosity blend with the warmth of your mouth, and there's a fresh balance of acidity and freshness.

WORD:	Snow
WINE:	Pinot Grigios, white Burgundies
BEER:	Flinty pilsners
FOOD:	Grilled fish, scallops in white wine, fresh pastas.

TAIHEIZAN KIMOTO *"Grand Mountain"*

Kimoto Junmai; Akita Prefecture; SMV: +/-ø; Acidity: 1.7. This is a traditional, pole-rammed sake that would appeal to the American palate. Welcoming and rich, it has a big, creamy nose with sides of banana and vanilla. It's soft and rolling, with expansive flavors hidden in a clean and delicate finish. A huge bite of flavor offers up all sorts of mouthfeel—chewy, syrupy, wide—with hints of nuts and a subtle backdoor fruitiness.

WORD:	Plush
WINE:	Pinot Noirs, hefty whites
BEER:	Chewy
FOOD:	Tomato-based dishes à la spaghetti and meatballs. Anything off the barbecue.

TAMANOHIKARI *"Brilliant Jade"*

Junmai Dai Ginjo; Kyoto Prefecture; SMV: +3.5; Acidity: 1.7. This is a very important dai ginjo to explore as this brewery uses the famous Omachi rice strain, the father of the majority of today's brewing rices. The nose, like its name, is indeed brilliant, filled with all sorts of peach, apple, and pear scents. Omachi rice yields deep and rich flavors, and this does not disappoint; you'll taste nuts and bananas to pears and cooked coconut meat. The viscous mouthfeel is chewy and plump. Despite an unmistakable fruitiness, the sake actually ends with dryness in the back of the throat.

WORD:	Pear
WINE:	Cabernets, white Burgundies
BEER:	Pilsners, mild stouts
FOOD:	Roasted birds (turkey, chicken, goose), as well as gamey meats and pâtés.

TENZAN *"Mount Tenzan"*

Junmai Genshu; Saga Prefecture; SMV: +2; Acidity: 1.7.
Mount Tenzan has a tantalizing nose filled with ripe
banana and strawberry tones. Flavors such as bananas,
melons, and crushed leaves run throughout the mouth in
a dry and solid transition. The viscosity and full-bodied
flavor would appeal to any red wine drinker with a
taste for flavor-forward sakes. Big flavor meets beautiful
packaging.

WORD:	Deep
WINE:	Rowdy reds, vast whites
BEER:	Stouts
FOOD:	Take-out sweet-and-sour pork, fried chicken, hot-pot dishes.

TSUKASABOTAN SENCHU HASSAKU
"Great Plan"

Junmai; Kochi Prefecture; SMV: +8; Acidity: −1.4. Great
Plan is one of those sakes that break the mold. It's quite
a dry brew, but it doesn't have the typical sharp, staccato
profile of a dry sake. Rather, it drinks clean and round
and provides a great example of a shimmering sake. The
nose is a collection of aromas from marshmallow and
cream to apple and plums. Hints of cherries and caramel
don't arrive until the dead-stop finish.

WORD:	Round
WINE:	Soft reds, dry whites
BEER:	Dry ales
FOOD:	Salty fare and guilty pleasures such as fish-and-chips.

UMENISHIKI *"Gorgeous Plum"*

Junmai Dai Ginjo; Ehime Prefecture; SMV: +2; Acidity:
1.4. This dai ginjo has an elegant nose of rose petals,
lychees, and strawberries and a flavor-forward rush of
melons, strawberries, and white peach. The taste is quite
complex, but a shimmery soft viscosity blends perfectly
with a muted acidity that produces a well-balanced
mouthful. For someone interested in exploring sake's
similarities to wine, this is a must.

WORD:	Layered
WINE:	Mellow Shirazes, chewy French whites
BEER:	Honey ales
FOOD:	Think candlelight dinner. Caviar, grilled asparagus, scallops in white wine.

UMENISHIKI SAKEHITOSUJI *"Gorgeous Plum"*

Junmai Ginjo Genshu; Ehime Prefecture; SMV: +1.5; Acidity: 1.9. Melon, cooked pears, and a dirty earthiness make up the nose on this genshu, and ripe fruit is almost swamped in a gooey and velvety full-bodied flavor with a finish that ends in a dead stop. High acidity makes it great for pairing with cooked fish. It's a great starter genshu in a user-friendly package.

WORD:	Pear
WINE:	Pinot Noirs, chewy dry whites
BEER:	Soft ales
FOOD:	Stellar with almost any cooked fish. Cream sauces work, as do dishes with gentle spice.

URAKASUMI *"Misty Bay"*

Junmai; Miyagi Prefecture; SMV: +2; Acidity: 1.3. From the moment this sake touches your lips to its departure down your throat, it maintains its balance. It has a subtle aroma of steamed rice and dried leaves, and at room temperature there are savory flavors with a wisp of chocolate. Served chilled, it has impressions of soft pear and mango. This is a sake that's perfectly comfortable with itself.

WORD:	Balanced
WINE:	Pinot Noirs
BEER:	Soft ales
FOOD:	Seafood pastas. Start with oysters on the half shell.

WAKATAKE ONIKOROSHI *"Demon Slayer"*

Junmai Dai Ginjo; Shizuoka Prefecture; SMV: +/- ø; Acidity: 1.4. With a nose of soft, ripe fruit and a tingle of citrus, this is one of the best-selling sakes in the United States for good reason. Tonalities of overly ripe cantaloupe and lychee swim in a silky flow from first sip to the well-built finish. It's a perfect example of a "round" sake, or one that blends flavor and acidity in equal proportions, and it's a tantalizing choice for those who appreciate a smooth move.

WORD:	Silky
WINE:	Shirazes, white Burgundies
BEER:	Crisp ales
FOOD:	Tropical fruits, fresh crab. Go wild with ceviche.

WAKATAKE ONIKOROSHI *"Demon Slayer"*

Junmai Ginjo; Shizuoka Prefecture; SMV: +3; Acidity:
1.5. The aroma on this ginjo is filled with sprightly
elements of watermelon and green veggies, but talk
about an expressive first sip: an explosion of chocolate,
grains, green apple, and minerals. The mouth speed is
quite slow, and this is made all the more enjoyable by an
abundance of fruit elements and sincere dryness. This is
a truly dependable choice that's great for beginners and
cherished by the well versed.

WORD:	Watermelon
WINE:	Pinot Noirs, dry Chardonnays
BEER:	Honey ales, ambers
FOOD:	Tomato-based dishes. Delivery pizza is perfect.

YAEGAKI *"Many Fences"*

Junmai Nigori; Hyogo Prefecture; SMV: -12; Acidity: 1.3.
This cloudy sake has a nose filled with *koji* rice, pear,
clover honey, and cinnamon. The very first sip tells you
this is a creamy nigori with a subtle sweetness balanced
by a good acidity. A very refreshing, pear-toned nigori,
it's an adventure for those looking for something creamy.

WORD:	Creamy
WINE:	Tannin-laced reds, expressive whites
BEER:	Creamy ales
FOOD:	Stands up to most spicy foods, such as fish tacos, but don't forget the cheese plate.

CHAPTER EIGHT

FOOD, MEET SAKE. SAKE, MEET FOOD.

THE SAKE REVOLUTION in Western culture has a final hurdle to clear—getting the public to accept the idea of pairing sakes with their favorite foods. Until now, most people's sake experiences have been limited to sushi restaurants; thus, sake and food have always been joined, but they have rarely gone beyond preparations of raw fish.

73

But there's hope. I was reminded the other day that wine only started to be taken seriously by Americans in the 1970s, around the same time vineyards started being planted in California. Since then, we've come a long way. Today, the concept of matching wines to foods has become a conversation unto itself. It's accepted that a glorious meal almost always requires a great accompanying wine.

I think we are just beginning to see sake in the same way, understanding that one doesn't need to be sitting at a sushi bar to drink sake. Ironically, the Japanese are witnessing a similar transformation. There, too, sake is being paired more and more with Western-inspired cuisine, shattering the idea that sake must be paired with Japanese food. In fact, when I was last in Japan, I ate out on three consecutive evenings in three different cities, and at each restaurant they had sake paired with risotto. These were not Italian restaurants either.

Sake has such a long history in Japan that I doubt if our notions of it will ever change completely. But here in the United States and elsewhere around the globe, chefs tinkering with fusion cuisine have been leading the way, pairing sake with foods that feel a little closer to home. Slowly but surely, we are seeing sake jump into the mix, from Peruvian restaurants to good, old-fashioned rib houses (check out Memphis Minnie's on Haight Street in San Francisco if you want a little sake with your barbecue). The cliché of sake—a piping hot beverage in a little ceramic jug—is being replaced by a wineglass filled with chilled sake parked right next to your housemade ravioli. In fact, sake has offered sommeliers a great pairing alternative when it comes to all sorts of modern Asian preparations, something that wine has had a difficult time doing.

Along with a few of my San Francisco friends—namely, Alain Rondelli, Eric Gower, and Jeff Inahara—Sara Deseran has created some dishes that are ideal for pairing with sake and are easy to make at home. There is a little bit of everything, from bar snacks to entrées that can stand alone. To help you along, we've paired a few of our fifty recommended sakes to try with each recipe.

Dare to Pair: General Rules for Food and Sake Pairing

THERE ARE NO RULES set in stone for pairing sake with food, just like it's not illegal to have a white wine with beef (it's actually a good idea sometimes). But there are some time-tested generalities that almost always do the trick, the main one being the bigger the flavor of the food, the bigger the sake.

As ginjo and dai ginjo sakes tend to be light and delicate, these are better paired with lighter and cleaner foods so the nuances of the sake do not get overwhelmed. When the recipe calls for robust, rich, seasoned, or creamy flavors, think junmai, and when you're serving up something clean, fragrant, light, refreshing, and smooth, think in the realms of ginjo or dai ginjo. (If all else fails, remember that junmais are the red wines of the sake world, as they have more backbone and structure.) And if your meal finds you at a sushi counter and the chef is Japanese, I recommend looking him in the eye and asking if he offers a sake from his hometown prefecture, and if not, order a drier ginjo.

Don't let the fear of frying keep you from making these beautifully lacy little chips (pictured on page 72). They're as simple as can be and the ideal thing to put out for a sophisticated cocktail party—that is, if you can keep from eating them hot out of the oil yourself. Fresh lotus root, which grows in sausagelike links, is available at Asian markets. SERVES 6 AS AN APPETIZER.

LOTUS ROOT CHIPS

1 pound fresh lotus root
Vegetable oil for deep-frying
Kosher salt to taste

SAKE
PAIRING SUGGESTIONS
Nishinoseki Junmai,
Wakatake Onikoroshi Junmai Ginjo,
Kan Chiku Junmai Dai Ginjo

Using a peeler, peel the links of the lotus root. Trim off the ends, and using a mandoline, slice the lotus root into rounds that are just a bit thicker than paper-thin. Place in water for 30 minutes in order to remove the starch. Strain, place on a tray, and pat dry with a towel.

Fill a wok or heavy-bottomed pot with at least 2 inches of oil. Use a deep-frying thermometer to gauge the heat of the oil. When it reaches 350°F, add the lotus root slices in batches, taking care not to overcrowd. Fry for about 90 seconds or until golden brown. Using a slotted spoon or shallow mesh strainer, remove to a paper towel–lined plate. Salt generously. Continue with the remaining lotus root slices.

The inspiration for these cashews came from chef James Ormsby of Jack Falstaff restaurant in San Francisco. Sweet and salty with a good spicy kick, they make a great bar snack.
MAKES 1 POUND.

CASHEWS WITH CURRY SALT

1 cup water

1 cup sugar

2 tablespoons Indian curry paste, such as Patak's Hot Curry Paste

1 pound raw whole cashews

½ tablespoon curry powder

½ tablespoon kosher salt

SAKE
PAIRING SUGGESTIONS
Fukunishiki Junmai,
Masumi Okuden Kantsukuri Junmai,
Shirakawago Nigori

Preheat the oven to 350°F. In a saucepan, bring the water and sugar to a boil and cook until it reaches 225°F with a candy thermometer, about 5 minutes. Be careful not to let the sugar burn or start to caramelize. Add the curry paste and stir well to combine.

Put the cashews in a bowl, add the sugar syrup, and stir to coat. Pour the mixture onto a baking sheet lined with a Silpat (a nonstick silicone mat available at cookware stores) or with parchment paper. Separate the nuts into a single layer and place the pan in the oven.

Bake the nuts about 30 minutes or until they are beginning to turn a golden brown. Take care not to overcook; nuts can burn within minutes. Meanwhile, in a bowl, mix the curry powder and salt together. Remove the nuts from the oven and toss in the bowl with the curry salt to taste. Spread the nuts on a greased sheet pan and separate them so they don't stick together. Let cool at room temperature. Store in an airtight container.

Glazed with an addictive combination of soy and sugar, and sprinkled with sesame seeds, these panfried sweet potato fries are as great for passing at a party as they are next to grilled pork chops. SERVES 4 TO 6 AS AN APPETIZER OR SIDE DISH.

SWEET POTATO FRIES WITH SOY-SUGAR GLAZE

1½ pounds sweet potatoes (about 3 medium) cut in half crosswise, skins left on

6 tablespoons peanut or canola oil

⅓ cup sugar

2 tablespoons soy sauce

¼ teaspoon salt

2 tablespoons water

¼ cup toasted sesame seeds

SAKE
PAIRING SUGGESTIONS
Hoyo Manamusume Junmai,
Bishonen Junmai Ginjo,
Kamoizumi Junmai Ginjo Nigori

Place the potatoes in a pot, cover with water, and bring to a boil. Let the potatoes boil until they are partially cooked, or a knife tip goes into them with some resistance, about 10 minutes. Drain and let cool. Peel and cut lengthwise into quarters. Cut those quarters into pieces that are the size of thick french fries, as similar in size as possible. Set aside.

Prepare a plate lined with paper towels and place it nearby. In a deep skillet over high heat, heat the peanut oil until almost smoking. In as many batches as necessary to avoid overcrowding, fry the sweet potatoes for about 6 to 8 minutes, taking care not to burn, using tongs to turn them so that they brown evenly on every side. Use a strainer or tongs to transfer them to the plate. Continue until the sweet potatoes are done.

Pour the oil into a disposable glass bottle or can (plastic will melt) and put the skillet back over high heat. When hot, add the sugar, soy sauce, salt, and water and stir to combine. Bring to a high boil. After a minute or so, when thick and bubbly, add all of the sweet potatoes and gently toss them in the soy-sugar glaze. Transfer to a serving plate. Sprinkle with sesame seeds and serve immediately.

Gravlax is one of the simplest things in the world to prepare but gives people the illusion that you're a celebrity chef. Although it's always cured using a combination of sugar and salt (usually in a ratio of one to one), after that, there aren't any rules. Here lemongrass and lemon zest add a citrusy element, and the sake gives it a delicate perfume. Although the gravlax is delicious plain, try slicing it thin and serving it on rice crackers; as a tea sandwich with wasabi mayonnaise; or most elegant of all, on a leaf of endive with a dollop of crème fraîche and a bit of wasabi caviar. Remember that gravlax is only as good as the salmon, so try to purchase wild salmon when it's in season and avoid farmed, otherwise known as Atlantic, salmon.
SERVES 6 TO 8 AS AN APPETIZER.

LEMONGRASS AND SAKE-CURED GRAVLAX

⅓ cup kosher salt

⅓ cup sugar

¼ cup peeled and finely chopped lemongrass

1½ teaspoons finely chopped lemon zest

1 pound center-cut wild salmon fillet, pinbones removed

2 tablespoons sake

SAKE
PAIRING SUGGESTIONS
Shirataki Jozen Junmai Ginjo, Manyou No Koubai Ginjo, Dassai Junmai Ginjo

In a small bowl, mix the salt, sugar, lemongrass, and lemon zest. Place a large piece of plastic wrap on a work surface and pour half of the salt mixture onto it. Place the salmon, skin side down, on top. Top the fillet with the remaining salt mixture and sprinkle with the sake, making sure the entire fillet is well covered. Tightly wrap the salmon up in the plastic wrap, sealing in the salt mixture. Wrap with plastic wrap again and place in a dish with a lip to catch any liquid that escapes.

Place the salmon in the refrigerator and place a weight on top, such as a bag of rice, to gently weigh it down. The next day, turn the salmon and replace the weight. Let the salmon cure a total of 3 days. Unwrap it, rinse off the salt mixture, pat it dry, and slice it thinly on an angle to serve, leaving the skin behind. (The skin can be dried and fried up for a snack.)

Once it is cured, the gravlax will keep, well wrapped in plastic, in the refrigerator for a week.

Served in little lettuce cups, this dish from Jeff Inahara, a San Francisco chef turned caterer, becomes the perfect first course. Black cod, as it's most commonly called, is also known as butterfish. But its true identity is actually sablefish. If you can't find it, try using salmon instead. Although not actually white in color, white miso is rice based and much sweeter than its more common red (also called brown) counterpart, so don't try to exchange the two. A yuzu is a Japanese citrus that has a flavor somewhere between a lemon and lime. The juice is available bottled online (try www.chefsresource.com) or at gourmet grocery stores.

Makes about 12; serves 6 as a first course.

MISO-MARINATED BLACK COD IN LETTUCE CUPS

1 pound boneless, skinless black cod (or salmon) fillet
1 cup white miso
⅔ cup sake
⅔ cup sugar

3 tablespoons mirin
1 tablespoon yuzu or lime juice
1 head butter lettuce
Toasted sesame seeds for sprinkling

SAKE
PAIRING SUGGESTIONS
*Daishichi Kimoto Shizenshu
Junmai, Umenishiki Sakehitosuji
Junmai Ginjo, Wakatake
Onikoroshi Junmai Dai Ginjo*

Cut the fish into 1½-ounce pieces, about 11 or 12 equal portions. Cover with plastic wrap and refrigerate while you prepare the miso marinade.

Combine the miso, sake, sugar, and mirin in a glass or stainless steel mixing bowl. Place over a pot of simmering water and cook until the sugar has dissolved and begins to caramelize, about 15 minutes. You will notice the miso start to darken. Stir occasionally to ensure even cooking, using a whisk if necessary to break up any clumps.

When the miso mixture is done, set aside and allow to cool. Cover and refrigerate until chilled. When chilled, stir in the yuzu juice. Gently fold the black cod into the marinade. Cover again and refrigerate overnight.

To prepare the fish, preheat a broiler. Core the butter lettuce and cut 12 cups out of the separated leaves using kitchen scissors. Wash and dry the lettuce cups. (Save the scraps for chopped salad.) Cover a baking sheet with aluminum foil and spray with nonstick spray. Evenly space the marinated cod onto the prepared baking sheet. Place under the broiler until the miso begins to caramelize, about 5 minutes. Watch carefully because the fish can burn easily.

Remove the fish from the oven and sprinkle with sesame seeds. Place a warm piece of cod into each lettuce cup and serve immediately.

Jeff Inahara's poke can be made the morning before it's served, as long as it's sealed well and stored in the refrigerator. For a more casual presentation, put the poke out in a bowl with a spoon with the fried wonton chips alongside. Shiso, also called parilla, is a member of the mint family and has large, jagged green (and sometimes purple) leaves. It is commonly found in Japanese markets. MAKES 30 APPETIZERS.

AHI-MANGO POKE WITH WONTON CHIPS

Peanut or canola oil for
   deep-frying
30 thin wonton wrappers
Kosher salt to taste
1 pound sashimi-quality ahi
   tuna, cut into ¼-inch dice
½ cup Japanese or English
   cucumber, cut into
   ¼-inch dice
½ cup ripe, but firm, mango,
   cut into ¼-inch dice
2 tablespoons minced shallot

2 tablespoons minced chives
2 tablespoons ichibiki tamari
   or soy sauce
2 tablespoons grape seed or
   canola oil
1 tablespoon seasoned rice
   wine vinegar
1 tablespoon peeled and
   grated fresh ginger
Freshly ground black pepper
   to taste
10 shiso leaves, finely torn

SAKE
PAIRING SUGGESTIONS
*Tenzan Junmai,
Kira Honjozo,
Koten Sharaku Junmai
Dai Ginjo*

Fill a deep, heavy pot or wok with about 1½ inches of oil, using a deep-frying thermometer to gauge the temperature, until it reaches 350°F. Set a wonton skin on a work surface and brush 2 adjacent edges of the wonton skin with water, folding over into a triangle and pressing to get rid of any air bubbles. Repeat with the remaining wonton wrappers. Allow to sit briefly before frying. Carefully drop the skins into the oil, about 5 at a time, cooking to a pale brown, about 45 seconds, using tongs to turn halfway through. Move to a cooling rack with a paper towel or newspaper beneath to catch the oil and season lightly with salt.

   In a bowl, add the tuna, cucumber, mango, shallot, and chives. In a separate bowl, whisk together the tamari, grape seed oil, rice wine vinegar, and grated ginger. Add a few turns of black pepper. Fold the dressing into the tuna mixture.

   Place one tablespoon of the poke onto each wonton chip. Garnish with the torn shiso leaves and serve.

81

Based on a recipe from Nina Simonds's wonderful book A Spoonful of Ginger, these bold, flavorful Chinese-style wings come out of the oven a gorgeous burnished color. They almost taste deep-fried, but the recipe doesn't call for a drop of oil. At such a high roasting temperature, the marinade can ruin a good baking sheet, so make sure to cover it well with foil. For cocktail-sized servings, just make the drumette part of the wings. SERVES 6.

ROASTED CHICKEN WINGS WITH GARLIC AND GINGER

1 cup soy sauce
1 cup sake
1 cup water
6 garlic chives or green
  onions, smashed
¼ cup sugar
8 cloves garlic, peeled
  and smashed

2-inch piece fresh ginger,
  sliced and smashed
3 ½ to 4 pounds chicken
  wings (about 20),
  rinsed and patted dry

SAKE
PAIRING SUGGESTIONS
*Gokyo Junmai,
Hitorimusume Junmai Nigori,
Senpuku Kura Junmai
Dai Ginjo*

To make the marinade, put the soy sauce, sake, water, garlic chives, sugar, garlic, and ginger into a saucepan. Bring to a boil, reduce to low, and simmer for 10 minutes. Let the marinade cool a bit.

With a knife or kitchen scissors, separate the drumettes from the wing tips at the joint. Place the chicken in a bowl and add the marinade. Coat well and cover with plastic wrap. Refrigerate and let marinate overnight.

Preheat the oven to 500°F. Line a baking sheet completely with foil and place the wings on it. Brush with more marinade. Roast for about 45 minutes or until the wings are cooked and crisp. Serve immediately with lots of napkins.

This refreshing and light salad is an example of perfect balance. It marries the sweet tartness of grapefruit with buttery crab and salty fried shallots, all with the backdrop of crisp, slightly bitter endive. Although everything, including the shallots (if they're stored in an airtight container), can be made the morning ahead, wait to toss it all together until it's time to serve.
Serves 4.

CRAB AND GRAPEFRUIT SALAD WITH FRIED SHALLOTS

FRIED SHALLOTS

1 cup peanut or canola oil
4 shallots, peeled, halved, and sliced

2 tablespoons all-purpose flour
Kosher salt to taste

DRESSING

1 tablespoon canola oil
2 tablespoons lime juice
1 tablespoon grapefruit juice
1 tablespoon fish sauce
2 teaspoons chopped jalapeño
½ teaspoon sugar

4 endives, rinsed
2 small pink grapefruit, segmented
1 pound crabmeat
¼ cup chopped cilantro

SAKE
PAIRING SUGGESTIONS
Urakasumi Junmai,
Kikusui Junmai Ginjo,
Sato No Homare Junmai Ginjo

Line a plate with paper towels and place it nearby. To make the fried shallots, heat the peanut oil in a pan until almost smoking. Toss the shallots in the flour, dust off well, and add to the oil in batches as necessary to avoid overcrowding. Fry for 5 minutes or until golden brown. Remove to the paper towel–lined plate. Sprinkle with salt and set aside.

To make the dressing, add the oil to a bowl and whisk in the lime juice, grapefruit juice, fish sauce, chopped jalapeño, and sugar.

Slice the endives in half lengthwise, core, and slice into long, wide slivers. Add them to a large serving bowl, along with the grapefruit, crab, and cilantro. Toss gently with the dressing. Top with the fried shallots and serve.

Part of the beauty of the slaw that accompanies these beef kebabs is its matchstick-crunchy texture. You don't have to have Martin Yan's knife skills to achieve perfect julienne—you just need a mandoline. While French mandolines can be very pricey, plastic Japanese mandolines are inexpensive and work perfectly well. Just make sure you watch your fingers when slicing. Serves 4.

GRILLED BEEF KEBABS WITH CUCUMBER-CARROT SLAW

2 teaspoons sugar
¼ cup soy sauce
1 teaspoon mirin

½ teaspoon chili sauce
1 pound thick rib-eye steak,
   cut into 1-inch cubes

SLAW

¾ pound English cucum-
   bers, peeled
¾ pound carrots, peeled
⅓ cup unseasoned rice
   wine vinegar

1 teaspoon kosher salt
1 teaspoon sugar

In a bowl, combine the sugar, soy sauce, mirin, and chili sauce. Add the beef, toss well, cover with plastic wrap, and place in the refrigerator for 2 hours to marinate.

Meanwhile, make the slaw. Slice the cucumbers into 4-inch lengths. Using a mandoline, slice these pieces into matchsticks. Place the sliced cucumber in a colander for about 20 minutes to allow any extra juice to drain. To slice the carrots, take an entire carrot and, pointing down at an angle, slice into matchsticks on the mandoline. (Throw the carrot stubs away if they get too hard to slice or if the blades get too close to your fingers.) In a small bowl, mix the vinegar, salt, and sugar. Add the carrots and cucumbers, toss well, cover with plastic wrap, and let marinate in the refrigerator for 2 hours. Let come to room temperature before serving.

To prepare the beef, thread the cubes onto bamboo skewers (soak the skewers first in water to keep them from burning). Prepare a grill. When it's very hot, place the skewers of beef on the grill and cook over direct heat for about 4 minutes, turning every minute or so. Remove from the grill and serve hot with a spoonful of the slaw alongside.

85

An elegant start to a meal, sake and clams are a typical Japanese pairing, but here a little but-
ter is used to enrich the broth. Although Kaffir lime—infused sake makes the dish even more
aromatic, it's perfectly delicious using noninfused sake too. Look for clams that are tightly
closed with no cracks. Serve by itself, with a bit of bread for sopping up the juice, or even try it
over noodles. SERVES 4.

SAKE-STEAMED CLAMS WITH GINGER

2 tablespoons butter
1 shallot, finely chopped
(about ¼ cup)
1-inch piece fresh ginger,
peeled and finely chopped
(about 2 tablespoons)
1 clove garlic, finely chopped
(about 1 tablespoon)
1 cup Kaffir lime—infused sake
(see page 99)

1 cup water
Kosher salt to taste
2 pounds live clams in the
shell, scrubbed clean
2 green onions, green parts
finely sliced

SAKE
PAIRING SUGGESTIONS
Tsukasabotan Senchu
Hassaku Junmai, Ozeki Osakaya
Chobei Dai Ginjo,
Daishichi Minowamon
Junmai Dai Ginjo

In a pot over medium heat, melt the butter. Add the shallot,
ginger, and garlic and cook until translucent, about 5 minutes.
Add the sake, water, and salt to taste (taking into consideration
the clams will release their juices, adding their briny flavor).
Bring to a simmer and let cook 5 more minutes.

Add the clams, cover, and simmer for 5 minutes or until the
clams open. Serve hot, scattered with green onions, placing an
empty bowl on the table for discarded shells.

This recipe was provided by Eric Gower, author of The Breakaway Japanese Kitchen. Eric, who lived in Japan for years, finds that already-shelled edamame, usually sold frozen, taste every bit as good when cooked as the ones sold in the pod, which tend to be much more expensive and require considerably more time to prepare. SERVES 4.

EDAMAME SALAD WITH SHISO AND MEYER LEMON VINAIGRETTE

3 cups shelled edamame, or soy beans (about 12 ounces)

2 Meyer lemons or regular lemons

5 shiso leaves, sliced into a chiffonade

3 tablespoons fruity extra-virgin olive oil

2 tablespoons rice vinegar

2 tablespoons maple syrup

Kosher salt to taste

Freshly ground black pepper to taste

SAKE
PAIRING SUGGESTIONS
Ichinokura Himezen Junmai, Dewazakura Dewasansan Junmai Ginjo, Hoyo Kura No Hana Junmai Dai Ginjo

Cook the edamame according to the package's instructions (the frozen kind are typically boiled for about 5 to 10 minutes). Drain, place in a serving bowl, and let cool to room temperature.

Zest 1 lemon and set aside. Squeeze the juice from the lemon (about 1 tablespoon plus 1 teaspoon). In a blender, add the lemon juice, half the shiso leaves, the olive oil, vinegar, and maple syrup. Add salt and pepper to taste. Blend well and gently mix the dressing with the edamame. Toss with the remaining shiso. Zest the other lemon and sprinkle the zest on top.

Although the Chinese use a form of bacon in many traditional dishes, for this nice wintry dish, the only Asian thing really is the shiitake mushrooms.   SERVES 4.

FETTUCCINE WITH SHIITAKE MUSHROOMS AND PANCETTA

3 tablespoons butter

2 tablespoons olive oil

3 ounces pancetta, chopped into 1-inch pieces (about ½ cup)

12 ounces shiitake mushrooms, stems removed, wiped clean, and sliced into ¼-inch pieces

¼ cup finely chopped carrot

6 sage leaves, chopped

1 teaspoon finely chopped garlic

½ cup cream

¼ teaspoon kosher salt or to taste

¼ teaspoon freshly ground black pepper or to taste

1⅓ pounds fresh or dried fettuccine

¼ cup finely chopped parsley

SAKE
PAIRING SUGGESTIONS
*Rihaku Junmai Nigori,
Meibo Yowano Tsuki Junmai Ginjo,
Harushika Junmai Dai Ginjo*

Heat 2 tablespoons butter and the olive oil in a medium-size skillet over medium heat. Add the pancetta and sauté for 2 minutes, stirring constantly. Add the mushrooms, carrot, sage leaves, and garlic. Sauté about 5 minutes, stirring occasionally. Add the cream, salt, and pepper and cook for another couple minutes, stirring.

Cook the pasta, according to instructions, in a large pot of well-salted, boiling water. When the pasta is al dente, remove from heat, drain, and mix with the remaining tablespoon butter.

Add the fettuccine to the pan with the mushroom sauce over medium heat and gently toss to combine. Sprinkle with the parsley and serve.

SAKE
PAIRING SUGGESTIONS
*Yaegaki Junmai Nigori,
Dewazakura Oka
Ginjo, Koshi No Tousetsuka
Junmai Ginjo*

There's no Latin-Japanese fusion going on here. (The word tacos, in this case, is simply supposed to give you an idea of how the food goes from hand to mouth.) This is a great way to have a casual make-your-own-sushi dinner party for a small group of friends. Rather than actually assembling the sushi ahead of time, set all of the ingredients on a communal platter and let everyone put whatever they want into pieces of nori (the seaweed), wrap it up—like a taco—and eat it just like that.
SERVES AS MANY AS YOU WANT; JUST INCREASE THE AMOUNT OF RICE AS NECESSARY.

SERVE-YOURSELF SUSHI TACOS

FOR THE RICE (ENOUGH FOR 6 PEOPLE)

2 cups sushi rice

**4 tablespoons unseasoned
rice vinegar**

2 tablespoons sugar

1 teaspoon kosher salt

Must-Have Basics: *Soy sauce, wasabi, pickled ginger, nori (using kitchen scissors, cut each sheet cut into four equal squares)*

Vegetarian Suggestions:
Cucumbers sliced into 2-inch sticks; slices of avocado; thinly sliced carrots; daikon sprouts; pickled daikon; cooked, sliced shiitake mushrooms; shiso leaves; cooked egg

Fish and Seafood Suggestions:
Cooked, peeled shrimp; raw sushi-grade ahi tuna cut into sushi-size pieces; flying fish or salmon roe; pieces of broiled unagi or eel (available frozen and already marinated at Japanese markets); real or imitation crabmeat; salmon (cooked or sushi-grade raw); cooked and sliced octopus

TO MAKE THE RICE

Wash the rice first by putting the rice in a pot or bowl of a rice cooker and add water to cover. Swirl a few times with your hand and drain, reserving the rice. Continue doing this until the water is clear. Drain. To cook, add 2¼ cups water to the rice. If using a pot, put the lid on and bring to a boil. Reduce to a simmer and cook until done, about 20 to 30 minutes. If using a rice cooker, turn it on and cook until the rice is done.

Meanwhile, in a small pot, add the rice vinegar, sugar, and salt. Bring to a simmer and cook until the sugar and salt dissolve. Remove from the heat and cool to room temperature. Add to the cooked rice, folding in gently. Let the rice cool to just warm before serving.

Artfully arrange all of the sushi ingredients on a platter and place the rice in a serving bowl with a top on it (or cover with a towel). Give everyone a small dipping bowl for soy sauce, but otherwise place everything in the middle of the table and let everyone use chopsticks to serve themselves.